The Appalachians

By Molly Aloian

🌳 Crabtree Publishing Company

www.crabtreebooks.com

Crabtree Publishing Company

www.crabtreebooks.com

Author: Molly Aloian
Editor: Adrianna Morganelli
Proofreader: Crystal Sikkens
Indexer: Wendy Scavuzzo
Designer: Katherine Berti
Photo researchers:
 Katherine Berti & Crystal Sikkens
Project coordinator: Kathy Middleton
**Production coordinator &
 prepress technician**: Katherine Berti

Front cover: Highlands, North Carolina, is a great
 spot for tourists looking to enjoy the beauty of
 the southern Appalachians.

Title page: The native flower, Flame Azalea, can be
 seen blooming along the Appalachian Trail in the
 Blue Ridge Mountains.

Picture credits:
Associated Press: p. 23, 41
Bridgeman Art Library: Peter Newark Western
 Americana: p. 35
Dreamstime: p. 21, 38
iStockphoto: p. 16 (farm), 20
Samara Parent: p. 5
Photo Researchers: Nicholas Bergkessel, Jr.: p. 45
Photos.com: p. 39
Bonna Rouse: p. 33
Shutterstock: cover, p. 1, 4, 6, 7 (top), 9, 10, 11, 12, 13, 14,
 15, 17, 18, 19, 22, 24, 25, 26, 27, 28, 29, 30, 31, 32, 36, 37,
 42, 43, 44
Thinkstock: p. 8
Wikimedia Commons: Daderot—Appalachian Mountain
 Club (AMC): p. 40; Pfly: p. 16 (map); William H.
 Powell (photograph courtesy Architect of the Capitol):
 p. 34; USDA Natural Resources Conservation Service:
 p. 7 (bottom)

Library and Archives Canada Cataloguing in Publication

Aloian, Molly
 The Appalachians / Molly Aloian.

(Mountains around the world)
Includes index.
Issued also in electronic formats.
ISBN 978-0-7787-7561-4 (bound).--ISBN 978-0-7787-7568-3 (pbk.)

 1. Appalachian Mountains--Juvenile literature. 2. Appalachian
Region--Juvenile literature. I. Title. II. Series: Mountains around
the world (St. Catharines, Ont.)

F106.A46 2011   j917.4   C2011-905233-4

Library of Congress Cataloging-in-Publication Data

Aloian, Molly.
 The Appalachians / Molly Aloian.
  p. cm. -- (Mountains around the world)
 Includes index.
 ISBN 978-0-7787-7561-4 (reinforced library binding : alk. paper) -- ISBN 978-
0-7787-7568-3 (pbk. : alk. paper) -- ISBN 978-1-4271-8842-7 (electronic PDF) --
ISBN 978-1-4271-9745-0 (electronic HTML)
 1. Natural history--Appalachian Mountains--Juvenile literature. 2.
Appalachian Mountains--History--Juvenile literature. 3. Appalachian
Mountains--Environmental conditions--Juvenile literature. 4. Mountain life--
Appalachian Mountains--Juvenile literature. I. Title. II. Series.

 QH104.5.A6A46 2012
 578.0974--dc23   2011029830

Crabtree Publishing Company

Printed in Canada/092011/MA20110714

www.crabtreebooks.com   1-800-387-7650

Published in Canada
Crabtree Publishing
616 Welland Ave.
St. Catharines, Ontario
L2M 5V6

Published in the United States
Crabtree Publishing
PMB 59051
350 Fifth Avenue, 59th Floor
New York, New York 10118

Published in the United Kingdom
Crabtree Publishing
Maritime House
Basin Road North, Hove
BN41 1WR

Published in Australia
Crabtree Publishing
3 Charles Street
Coburg North
VIC 3058

CONTENTS

Words that are defined in the glossary are in **bold** type
the first time they appear in the text.

CHAPTER 1

The Appalachian Mountains

The Appalachians are a mountain range in the eastern part of North America. They are among the oldest mountains on Earth. They extend almost 2,000 miles (3,218 km) from the Canadian province of Newfoundland and Labrador all the way down to Alabama in the United States. The Appalachians form a natural barrier between the eastern **coastal plain** and the interior lowlands of North America.

The Western Brook Pond on the west coast of Newfoundland is a fjord, or long, narrow inlet surrounded by steep walls made of rock. The walls of this fjord are 2,000 feet (600 m) high.

Playing Their Part

The Appalachians have played an important role in the history of North America. Long ago, people survived in the mountains by growing crops on the lush farmland and raising animals. Eventually, the trees and other **natural resources** became the basis for the **economy** in the Appalachians. For hundreds of years, the mountains acted as a natural barrier for the westward expansion of European **colonists** who were exploring North America. The French and Indian War, the **American Revolution**, and the American Civil War all took place among the Appalachian Mountains.

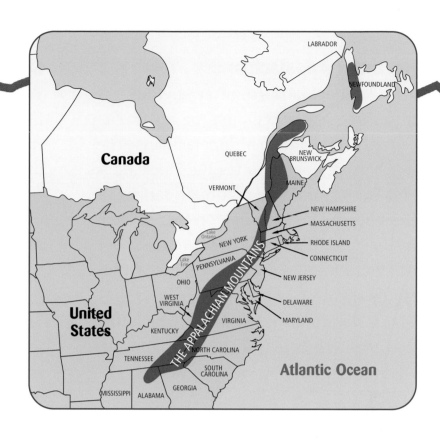

What is a Mountain?

A mountain is a gigantic natural landform that rises above Earth's surface. A mountain often has steep sides rising to a summit, which is the highest point or peak. Mountains are usually found in long ranges or groups of ranges called chains. They are formed in different ways, but most of the mountains on Earth have formed over millions of years. You may not be able to notice or feel it, but mountains are forming even as you read this book!

NOTABLE QUOTE

"The Appalachian Mountains are some of the oldest mountains on Earth…[the mountains] have shaped the lives of the people who live there—and such is still the case today."

—Sacred Rides Mountain Bike Adventures

Northern Appalachians

The Appalachians are often divided into three major regions: the northern, central, and southern Appalachians. The northern region includes the Shickshocks and the Notre Dame mountain ranges in Quebec, the Long Range on the island of Newfoundland, the great monadnock of Mount Katahdin in Maine, the White Mountains in New Hampshire, and the Green Mountains in Vermont, which turn into the Berkshire Hills in Massachusetts, Connecticut, and eastern New York.

Central Appalachians

The central Appalachians include New York's Catskill Mountains, as well as the beginnings of the Blue Ridge mountain range in southern Pennsylvania and the Allegheny Mountains, which rise in southwestern New York and cover parts of western Pennsylvania, western Maryland, and eastern Ohio before merging south. The central Appalachians also include the Alleghenies of West Virginia and Virginia, the Blue Ridge mountain range, the Unaka Mountains in southwestern Virginia, eastern Tennessee, and western North Carolina, and the Cumberland Mountains. The Great Smoky Mountains are part of the Unaka Mountains.

Southern Appalachians

The southern Appalachians boast the highest mountains in the Appalachian range. Maine's Mount Katahdin is over 5,000 feet (1,524 m) and New Hampshire's Mount Washington is over 6,000 feet (1,829 m). Peaks in the White Mountains rise above 5,000 feet (1,524 m). The peaks of the Black Mountains and the Great Smoky Mountains rise above 6,000 feet (1,829 m). The highest summit is Mount Mitchell.

Kaaterskill Falls, located in the eastern Catskill Mountains of New York, is a waterfall made up of two cascades that total 260 feet (79 m) in height.

Mount Katahdin is the highest mountain in Maine. It measures 5,268 feet (1,606 m) high, and was formed from underground magma.

FAST FACT

The Appalachian Mountains form part of the same mountain range as the Atlas Mountains of Morocco and Algeria. This is because millions of years ago, the continents of North America and Africa were joined together in one large landmass.

The highest peak in the Appalachians is Mount Mitchell, which is in North Carolina. Mount Mitchell is 6,684 feet (2,037 m) above sea level.

Mountain Exploration

Indigenous people had been living in the Appalachian Mountains for thousands of years before European colonists settled in the region. Today, many people live and work in mountain towns and villages in the Appalachians. Tourists and vacationers also visit the mountains to witness their breathtaking beauty and wildlife. Great Smoky Mountains National Park, on the border of Tennessee and North Carolina, is one of the most visited national parks in the United States. More than nine million people visit the park each year.

FAST FACT

Around one million years ago, Earth's **climate** cooled a few degrees. Huge glaciers, or sheets of ice, formed in Arctic regions and slowly moved south over North America and Eurasia. These glaciers formed and then melted four more times. These time periods are known as glaciations or ice ages.

The Mohonk Mountain House is a resort in the Appalachian mountains in New York. Tourists visit this Victorian castle for its scenery and to enjoy hiking trails, boating, cross-country skiing, snowshoeing, and various other activities.

Appalachian Adaptations

Thousands of animals, including black bears, moose, white-tailed deer, foxes, beavers, and raccoons, live throughout the Appalachians. Their bodies are **adapted** to the mountain conditions. Different types of trees and other plants grow at different **elevations**. Coniferous trees or evergreens can grow at high elevations because they are adapted to cold winters and short growing seasons. The highest altitude at which trees can survive is called the tree line.

Many raccoons live in the forests of the Appalachian Mountains.

Many Mountains

There are mountains all over Earth on every single continent and in nearly every single country. Approximately 20 percent of the total land area on Earth is made up of mountains. There are even underwater mountain ranges. The Mid-Atlantic Ridge, the longest mountain range on Earth, extends through the Atlantic Ocean. The Mid-Atlantic Ridge forms a giant letter C between South America and Africa.

FAST FACT

Mountains are home to at least 12 percent of the world's population. More than 70 million people live above altitudes of 6,500 feet (1,981 m). Another 14 percent live very close to mountain areas and over half of the world's population depends on mountains for water, food, **hydroelectricity**, **timber**, and **mineral** resources.

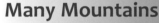

9

CHAPTER 2

How Did the Appalachians Form?

The Appalachian Mountains are very old mountains. They are older than the Himalayas, the Rockies, and the Alps. The Appalachians began forming over 480 million years ago. Today, geologists are very interested in studying the Appalachians. Geologists are scientists who study the structure of Earth and how Earth formed.

Linville Gorge, shown here, is sometimes called the Grand Canyon of North Carolina. It is part of the Pisgah National Forest. The gorge was first designated as a protected wild area in 1951.

Moving Plates

The Earth's crust is divided into giant slabs of rock called **tectonic plates**. These plates do not stay in the same place. They are constantly moving, which causes earthquakes and volcanic eruptions on Earth. They move very slowly, but the changes on Earth can be enormous. As they slowly move, the plates sometimes push up against one another. This causes their edges to slowly force up into gigantic folds and wrinkles, becoming what we know as mountains. The Appalachian Mountains were formed in this way. However, in order to completely understand the process we must go back in time hundreds of millions of years.

FAST FACT

The formation of mountains is called orogenesis.

Earth's Layers

Earth is made up of different layers of rock. The outermost layer of Earth is called the crust. Below the crust is the mantle, which is a very thick, dense layer of rock. The mantle is approximately 1,800 miles (2,897 km) thick—much thicker than the crust. The outer core is the next layer. The temperature of the outer core is very hot, but the inner core is even hotter. The temperature of the inner core is about 9,000°F (4,982°C).

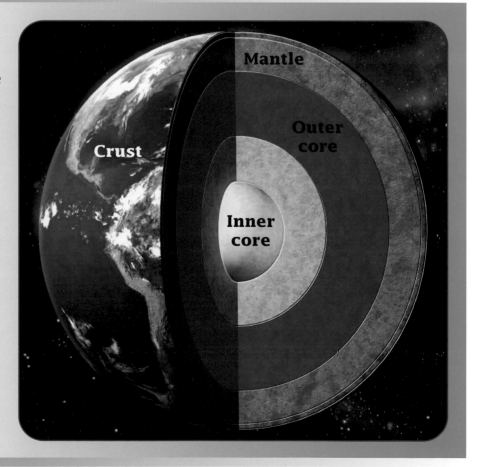

Crust

Mantle

Outer core

Inner core

Layers of Sediment

More than one billion years ago, all of the continents on Earth were joined together in one **supercontinent** surrounded by one giant ocean. About 750 million years ago, the crust of the supercontinent began to pull apart. As the crust broke apart, a deep **basin**, called the Ocoee, formed in what is now the western Carolinas, eastern Tennessee, and northern Georgia. Ocean water filled the basin, and layers and layers of sediment—clay, silt, sand, and gravel—were deposited on the bottom. Millions of years passed and an extremely thick layer of sediment accumulated. Today, this sediment forms the **bedrock** of the Great Smoky Mountains.

Drifting Away

As sediment continued to accumulate, volcanoes erupted in present-day Virginia, North Carolina, South Carolina, and Georgia. **Lava** from some volcanoes flowed in slow-moving sheets, but some eruptions were explosive. About 540 million years ago, the supercontinent split into pieces that drifted away from each other. Seawater spread into low areas between plates and, in time, formed new oceans that continued to expand. A shallow sea covered most of the present-day United States. During that time, algae, bacteria, and many species of **invertebrates** lived in the oceans, but there were no plants or animals living on land.

Many sections along the Little Pigeon River in the Great Smoky Mountains National Park show exposed bedrock.

Continental Collision

About 470 million years ago, the direction of the plates changed and began to move toward each other. As the continental plates moved closer together, pieces of oceanic crust, islands, and other landmasses collided with the eastern part of present-day North America. By this time, there were plants on land, followed soon after by scorpions, insects, and amphibians.

At one time, all the continents on Earth were joined as one large landmass known as Pangea.

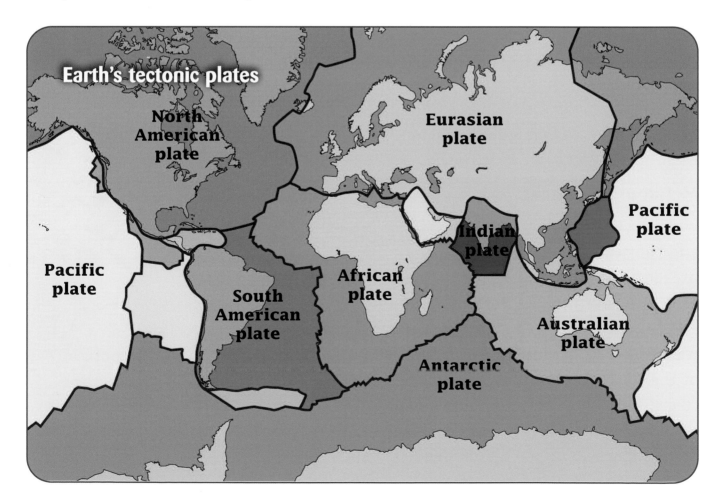

Earth's tectonic plates

North American plate

Eurasian plate

Pacific plate

Pacific plate

South American plate

African plate

Indian plate

Australian plate

Antarctic plate

Pile Up

About 270 million years ago, there was a second collision. The tectonic plates carrying North America and Africa collided. Huge masses of rock were pushed westward along the edge of present-day North America. There were also massive earthquakes. As the masses of rock collided, they piled up to form the mountains that we know today as the Appalachians. Today, the Atlantic Ocean is still becoming wider. The ocean's crust is pulling apart at the mid-Atlantic Ridge.

Igneous Rocks

As blocks of Earth's crust passed across one another, some rocks became so hot that they melted. Molten rock at Earth's surface erupts to form either explosive volcanoes or quiet lava flows. When molten rock remains deep underground, it cools and **crystallizes** to form **igneous rocks** called plutons. Igneous plutons are scattered throughout the southern Appalachians. Looking Glass Rock, which is south of Asheville, North Carolina, is an igneous pluton.

Most of the rocks in the Smoky Mountains, which are located along the border of Tennessee and North Carolina, are made up of metamorphic rocks.

Metamorphic Rocks

When tectonic plates, islands, and the sea floor collided with present-day North America, the force of the collision caused extreme pressure and heat. In some places, the temperature was very high, but below the melting point of the rocks. Here, the rocks deformed and re-crystallized to become **metamorphic rocks**. There are metamorphic rocks in many places along the Blue Ridge Parkway in North Carolina and Virginia.

FAST FACT

Metamorphic rocks re-crystallize in sheets that split easily into thin, smooth layers. These rocks are perfect for skipping off the banks of rivers or creeks. Their flat, smooth shape allows them to skip easily across the surface of the water.

Looking Glass Rock was named for the way the sunshine reflects off of its granite face.

Mountain Migration

The Great Smoky Mountains are among the oldest mountains in the world. Species **migrated** along their slopes during climatic changes such as the last ice age, 10,000 years ago. In fact, the glaciers of the last ice age affected the Smoky Mountains without invading them. During that time, glaciers scoured much of North America but did not quite reach as far south as the Smoky Mountains.

The Great Smoky Mountains National Park encompasses 814 square miles (2,108 square km), making it one of the largest protected areas in the eastern United States.

The Great Valley

One distinctive feature of the Appalachian Mountains is the Great Appalachian Valley. The valley is like a gigantic **trough**. It stretches 1,200 miles (1,931 km) from Quebec to Alabama. Indigenous people were the first to use routes through the valley.

There is lush farmland in the valley, especially in the Cumberland and Shenandoah valleys. For European colonists, the Great Appalachian Valley was a major route for settlement and **commerce** in the United States.

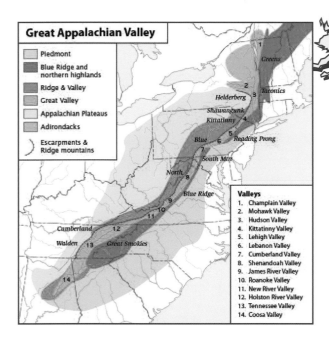

Great Appalachian Valley

- Piedmont
- Blue Ridge and northern highlands
- Ridge & Valley
- Great Valley
- Appalachian Plateaus
- Adirondacks
- Escarpments & Ridge mountains

Greens
Taconics
Helderberg
Shawangunk
Kittatinny
Blue
Reading Prong
South Mtn
North
Blue Ridge
Cumberland
Walden
Great Smokies

Valleys
1. Champlain Valley
2. Mohawk Valley
3. Hudson Valley
4. Kittatinny Valley
5. Lehigh Valley
6. Lebanon Valley
7. Cumberland Valley
8. Shenandoah Valley
9. James River Valley
10. Roanoke Valley
11. New River Valley
12. Holston River Valley
13. Tennessee Valley
14. Coosa Valley

FAST FACT

The Museum of the Shenandoah Valley opened in 2005. It highlights the region's art, culture, and history. Located in Winchester, Virginia, it is part of a complex that also features gardens and a historic house.

There are many horse farms scattered throughout the fertile Shenandoah Valley.

The Hudson River runs through the Hudson River Valley, which is part of the Great Appalachian Valley. The river flows 315 miles (507 km) from north to south through eastern New York.

Worn Down

As soon as any mountain forms, rainwater and freezing temperatures slowly wear the mountain down. This process is called erosion. Rivers carve deep valleys into rocks. Wind blows soil and small bits of rocks away. When water freezes inside a crack in a mountain rock, it expands. This expansion forces the rock to split apart and break into smaller pieces, slowly chipping away at the mountain. For the last 100 million years, erosion has carved away the Appalachians. At the time they formed, the Appalachians were jagged and much higher than they are now. They were once similar in height to the Rocky Mountains.

CHAPTER 3
Weather in the Appalachians

The weather in the Appalachian Mountains varies greatly from north to south. For example, the climate in the northernmost parts of the mountain range is **subarctic**, while ranges throughout Georgia and Alabama have milder climates.

A storm sweeps over Shenandoah Valley in the Blue Ridge Mountains of Virginia.

This mountain in the Great Smoky Mountains National Park is capped in snow with autumn foliage at the lower elevations.

Varying Temperatures

The temperatures and rainfall in the Appalachians vary according to region and elevation. For example, average annual temperatures range from below 50°F (10°C) in the north to approximately 64°F (17.7°C) at the south end of the mountains. Average annual precipitation varies from 35 inches (89 cm) in the valleys to 80 inches (203 cm) on the highest peaks. Slopes facing the south and southeast are notably warmer and drier than slopes facing north and northwest because they face the Sun.

Hot and Cold

Parts of Quebec and Newfoundland and Labrador have a subarctic climate. A subarctic climate consists of long, bitterly cold winters and short, cool summers. This means that the growing season is also very short. The variations in temperature can be extreme. For example, in summer, daytime temperatures can rise to 77°F (25°C) and then drop down to 50°F (10°C) in the evening.

Water Droplets

Precipitation, including rain, snow, sleet, and hail, is higher on mountains than in lowlands. Water **evaporates** from oceans and other bodies of water. The moist air moving toward mountains is forced to rise upward. This air becomes cool and forms clouds. Water droplets within the clouds move around and eventually collide with each other and form larger droplets. When they are large enough, the droplets fall to the ground as rain or snow.

Frost At Night

Frost occurs often in the Appalachians. Small ice crystals form on the ground when the temperature drops below freezing, usually at night. The average length of the frost-free period is about 100 days in the northern mountains, and about 220 days in the low southern parts of the Appalachians. Frost heaving occurs when an area of water between layers of rock freezes, expands, and then lifts a whole section of rock clear of the surrounding layers. The rock is placed back down as the ice melts. Unique and interesting rock shapes are often created from frost heaving.

FAST FACT

About 20,000 years ago, glaciers covered 16 million square miles (42 million square km) of Earth. Earth's glaciers are slowly melting because of **global warming**. Today, only six million square miles (15.5 million square km) of Earth is covered in ice. There are no permanent glaciers in the Appalachians.

Frost can be seen covering the landscape on winter mornings in the Great Smoky Mountains.

Weather stations, like this one on Mount Washington, are equipped with instruments to observe atmospheric conditions for forecasting the weather as well as to study the climate.

Hard to Study

It is difficult for people to study the climate on mountains. Many mountainous regions are remote and there are no people living nearby. As a result, it is expensive to install and maintain weather stations. Mountainous regions also have an extremely wide variety of weather conditions at summits, on slopes, and in valleys. Any weather station would be representative of the weather in only a limited range of places.

The Mount Washington Observatory monitors the weather at the rocky, windswept summit of Mount Washington in New Hampshire. The observatory's mission is to help people understand the natural systems that create Earth's weather and climate. The organization maintains its mountaintop weather station, conducts research and educational programs, and interprets the heritage of the Mount Washington region.

Snowfalls

The heaviest snow in the Appalachians occurs on the upslope side of the higher mountain ridges along the border between North Carolina and Tennessee, and the border between Virginia and West Virginia. Mountain regions in Pennsylvania can receive more than 24 inches (61 cm) of snow. This amount can increase to approximately 30 inches (76 cm) southward in the Smoky Mountains. It snows more frequently in the higher mountains and up to two feet (0.6 m) can fall during a storm. January and February are the snowiest months in the Appalachians.

Winters in Webster County, West Virginia, are cold and snowy.

Stormy Weather

In November of 1950, a terrible storm blew through the eastern United States including the Appalachians. The storm caused winds and heavy rains just east of the Appalachians and blizzard conditions along the western slopes of the mountains. Winds on Mount Washington reached more than 160 miles per hour (257 km per hour). More than one million people lost power and more than 300 people died during the storm.

Cars in Pittsburg, Pennsylvania, were completely covered with snow during the storm.

Hot Stuff

Global warming is the increase in the average temperature of Earth. Research has shown that the average air temperature in the United States has increased by about 1°F (0.6°C) over the last 100 years. Scientists estimate that temperatures will increase 5.4°F to 9°F (3°C-5°C) over the next century, causing waterways to heat up, too. Global warming affects the delicate balance of life in the Appalachian Mountains including the flow of Appalachian streams. Bigger floods and warmer, slower-moving streams will harm the brook trout and other fish that are native to the Appalachians. This will, in turn, affect the animals that feed on the fish.

CHAPTER 4

Plants and Animals

The Appalachians are home to hundreds of thousands of species of plants and animals. Trees, shrubs, wildflowers, and animals, including many species of birds, fish, reptiles, and insects, live throughout the mountains.

The Trillium flower is native to the Smoky Mountains area.

Tons of Trees

There are hundreds of species of trees in the Appalachians. Conifers, including the red spruce and balsam fir, grow on the highest parts of the Appalachians. Other trees include the yellow birch, American beech, mountain maple, hobblebush, and pin cherry, as well as sugar maple, scarlet oak, sweetgum, red maple, and hickory trees. As summer ends, the green **pigments** in leaves diminish and the leaves change color. The pigments that make carrots orange and leaves yellow, called carotenoids, are exposed as the green in the leaves fades. Reds and purples come from pigments called anthocyanins. These pigments are formed when sugars in leaves break down in bright autumn sunlight.

Spring Flowers

In late winter and early spring, a group of flowers called **ephemerals** start to appear above ground. These flowering plants emerge from February to April and are **dormant** by May or June. They produce flowers, fruits, and die within a two-month period. The ephemerals appear before deciduous trees have their full leaves, when plenty of sunlight is streaming onto the forest floor. During this time, there is a lot of moisture and **nutrients** in the soil from the **decomposing** tree leaves that fell the previous autumn. Spring ephemerals include flowers such as trilliums, lady's slipper orchids, crested dwarf iris, fire pink, columbines, bleeding heart, phacelia, jack-in-the-pulpits, little brown jugs, and violets.

FAST FACT

Appalachian shrubs with beautiful flowers include the rhododendron, azalea, and mountain laurel.

The carotenoids are exposed on these sugar maple leaves.

Yellow Lady's Slipper is an orchid that grows at Smoky Mountain.

There are many waterfalls in the Appalachian Mountains. Water trickles or rushes down the mountainsides, from high elevations to low, sometimes dropping more than one mile (1.6 km) in elevation from the high peaks to the foothills.

Under Attack

Eastern hemlock trees are among the largest and most common trees in the Appalachians. They can grow to be more than 150 feet (46 m) tall and have trunks that are more than six feet (1.8 m) in diameter. Unfortunately, a dangerous insect called the woolly adelgid is attacking the trees. The woolly adelgid feeds on the sap at the base of hemlock needles, which stops the flow of nutrients to the needles. Eventually, the needles change from deep green to a grayish green, then fall off. Without needles, the trees cannot get the nutrients they need and usually die within three to five years. **Infestations** often start in large, mature hemlocks, but the insects also attack and kill younger trees as well.

Full Bloom

In summer, bright red cardinal flowers, pink turtleheads, Turk's-cap lily, small purple-fringed orchids, bee balm, butterfly weed, black-eyed Susans, jewelweed, and many other flowers are in full bloom. By late summer and through the fall, goldenrod, wide-leaved sunflowers, tall ironweed, mountain gentians, monkshood, coneflowers, and many species of asters begin to bloom. Purple clusters of sweet Joe-Pye weed can reach heights of 10 feet (3 m).

FAST FACT

Great Smoky Mountains National Park is a world-renowned reserve of wildflower diversity. There are over 1,660 kinds of flowering plants in the park, more than in any other North American national park.

In fact, the park is sometimes referred to as the Wildflower National Park.

Turk's-cap lily

goldenrod

bee balm

These rhododendrons are blooming along the Blue Ridge Parkway near Ashville, North Carolina.

Animals of All Kinds

Appalachian animals include tree squirrels, rabbits, white-tailed deer, moose, elk, beavers, skunks, foxes, wolves, and black bears. Birds including wild turkeys, grouse, mourning doves, ravens, wood ducks, great horned owls, and a wide variety of songbirds also make their homes in the Appalachian Mountains.

No Lungs

Different species of salamanders live in the Appalachians at elevations up to 3,000 feet (914 m). One species, called lungless salamanders, do not have lungs. They take in **oxygen** through the walls of tiny blood vessels in their skin and linings of their mouths and throats. Lungless salamanders live in and along streams and under rocks, logs, and **leaf litter** in the forests. There are more than 20 species of lungless salamanders living in the Appalachians. Lungless salamanders use their tongues to capture small prey, including insects and small worms, while other salamanders capture their prey by grasping them in their jaws.

The meadows of the Appalachians are home to wild turkeys.

Wood ducks live near water in the Appalachians. They can also be found in trees where they build their nests, rest, and preen.

The long-tail salamander is just one of many lungless salamander species that live in the Appalachians' forests.

Black bears can grow to be six feet (1.8 m) in length and up to three feet (0.9 m) high at the shoulder.

Black Bears

Thousands of black bears live in the Appalachians. During the summer months, male bears weigh approximately 250 pounds (113 kg), while female black bears are generally smaller and weigh just over 100 pounds (45 kg). However, bears can double their weight by the fall. Some bears weigh over 600 pounds (272 kg) in the fall.

Black bears are **omnivores**. Plants, berries, and nuts make up approximately 85 percent of their diet. Insects and animal **carrion** provide valuable sources of protein for bears. American black bears often mark their territory and dominance by biting or clawing trees five to seven feet (1.5 to 2.1 m) up the trunks. The bear with the highest claw or bite mark on the tree is dominant in the area.

Oh, Deer!

White-tailed deer live throughout the Appalachians, but are most commonly found in areas with open fields. The many plants in the Appalachians provide plenty of food for white-tailed deer. Coyotes, black bears, and bobcats prey on white-tailed deer, especially young fawns. The coat of a white-tailed deer fawn is marked with white spots to provide camouflage from these predators. The spots help the fawn blend in with its surroundings so it is harder for predators to see.

A coyote stalks its prey through a grassy meadow.

The tall grass and the spotted coat of this fawn help to keep it hidden from predators.

A bobcat is looking for rabbits and other small animals to eat.

Back In Town

Elk once roamed in the southern Appalachian Mountains and throughout the eastern United States. They disappeared from the region as a result of over-hunting and loss of habitat. The experimental release of elk into the Great Smoky Mountains National Park began in 2001. The land between the Lakes National Recreation Area along the Tennessee-Kentucky border brought in 25 elk. One year later, the park imported another 27 elk. In 2009 and 2010, the park began developing an environmental assessment of the program and a long-term management plan for the elk. Partners in the project include the Rocky Mountain Elk Foundation, Parks Canada, Great Smoky Mountains Natural History Association, Friends of the Smokies, the U.S.G.S. Biological Resources Division, and the University of Tennessee.

FAST FACT

Willfully getting within 150 feet (46 m) of elk or doing anything that disturbs or displaces elk in their habitats is illegal in the Great Smoky Mountains National Park. Violation of this rule can result in fines and arrest.

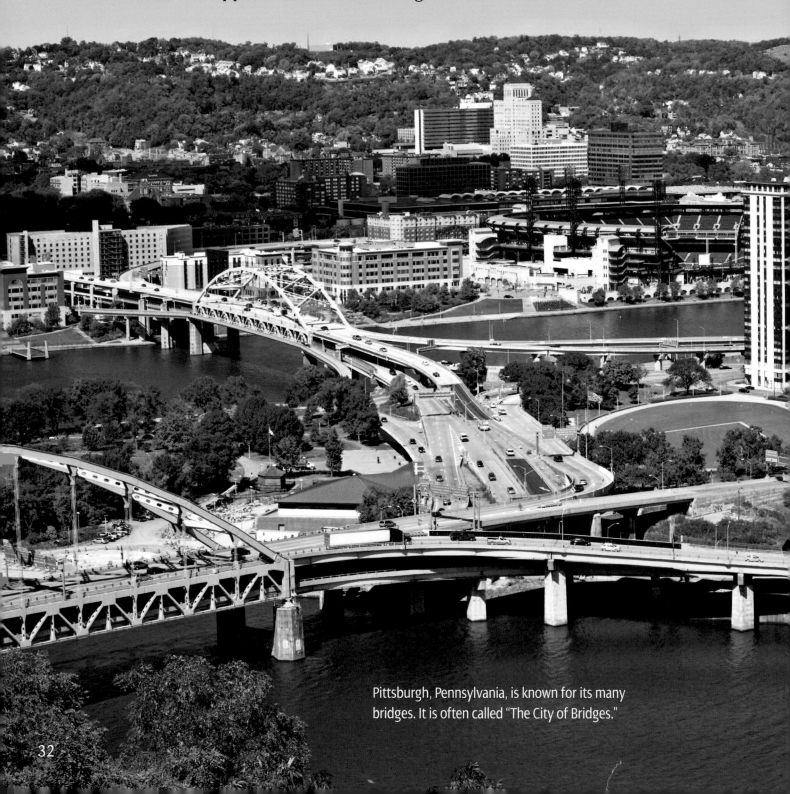

CHAPTER 5
People in the Appalachians

People have been living in the Appalachian Mountains for thousands of years. The region's original inhabitants were indigenous peoples, including the Cherokee, Chickasaw, and Choctaw. Today, over 20 million people live in towns and cities in the Appalachian Mountain region.

Pittsburgh, Pennsylvania, is known for its many bridges. It is often called "The City of Bridges."

Hunters and Fishers

Indigenous peoples lived in the Appalachians as early as 8000 B.C. These people are known as Paleo-Indians. They were hunters. They hunted large animals such as **mammoths**. Over time, the Paleo-Indians and their **descendants** developed new ways of life using the natural resources they found in the mountains. Several distinctive Native cultures emerged in the region during the subsequent centuries. Long before European settlement, the Pennacook, Mohican (Mahican), and Susquehanna lived in the northern half of the Appalachians. The Cherokee lived mainly in the southern mountains. These people hunted animals, such as deer and elk, in the mountains and caught fish in the waterways.

Nancy Ward, a Cherokee woman who lived in present-day Tennessee, is famous for trying to maintain peaceful relations between her people and the U.S. government.

Mysterious Mountains

During the 1500s, European explorers and settlers began to enter the Appalachian region. The mountains acted like a huge barrier, however. The terrain was extremely rugged and difficult to access, and the explorers were frustrated by the size and complexity of the mountain ranges. Many of the streams and rivers were difficult to navigate. The dense mountain forests were another challenge the explorers had to face. The central Appalachians had waterways that were easier to get across, so this area attracted the most settlers.

FAST FACT

The traditional territory of the Cherokee spanned several present-day states, including North Carolina, Kentucky, Tennessee, Virginia, South Carolina, Georgia, and Alabama.

33

Defending Territories

In 1539, the Spanish explorer named Hernando de Soto entered the Appalachian region. De Soto and his army encountered the Cherokee. Cherokee warriors tried to defend their traditional territories against the Spanish and other European settlers and explorers. Their traditional cultures were very different from European ways of living and thinking, however.

Striking Gold

The discovery of gold caused many changes in the Appalachian Mountains. In 1829, newspaper articles described vast riches of gold in Cherokee territory in Georgia. Thousands of European miners rushed to the area with dreams of becoming rich. They washed gravel from banks of the streams to search for gold. The Cherokee people living in the region knew about the gold, but it did not have the same significance for them as it did for the new settlers.

Hernando de Soto and his Spanish companions were the first Europeans to view the Mississippi River. The European settlers forced their traditions, such as their religion and culture, onto the Native people that were living there.

Trail of Tears

In the early 1800s, following the American Revolution, American people did not want the Cherokee and other Native people living on the lands Americans had claimed as their own. In 1830, the United States government passed the Indian Removal Act, which forced all the Native people to move. Between 1830 and 1840, more than 60,000 Cherokee, Chickasaw, Choctaw, Creek, and other Native people were forced to leave their traditional territories. They were forced to move to Indian Territory, which was an area of land west of the Mississippi River that was allotted for Native people. This relocation of the Native nations is known as "The Trail of Tears."

FAST FACT

Approximately 1,400 Cherokee people escaped "The Trail of Tears" by hiding in the Smoky Mountains. Ultimately, the federal government allowed them to live there. Today, the descendants of this group of Cherokee still live in the Smoky Mountains and tourists can visit a section of the Cherokee territory.

For thousands of people, the journey to Indian Territory was over 1,000 miles (1,609 km) long, and many people died from starvation and exhaustion along the way.

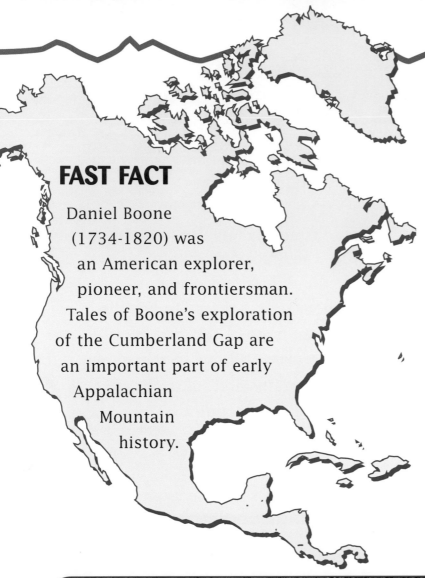

Daniel Boone (1734-1820) was an American explorer, pioneer, and frontiersman. Tales of Boone's exploration of the Cumberland Gap are an important part of early Appalachian Mountain history.

A Distinct Place

Today, there are numerous cities, towns, and villages throughout the Appalachian Mountains. There are businesses, schools, churches, and shopping centers, as well as many parks and recreational areas. Roads and highways connect the smaller mountain towns and villages to the bigger cities within the valleys. Many of the people living in the Appalachians claim that it is one of the geographic regions of the United States with its own distinct culture, including music, handicrafts, **folklore**, religious practices, social customs, and traditions.

The famous hiking trail, Appalachian Trail, runs through the historic town of Harpers Ferry in West Virginia.

Great Appalachian Trail

The Appalachian Trail, also known as the A.T., is the longest continuously marked footpath in the world, measuring roughly 2,180 miles (3,508 km) in length. The trail spans through 14 states along the crests and valleys of the Appalachians. It runs from the northern point at Katahdin, in Maine, to the trail's southern end at Springer Mountain, in Georgia.

NOTABLE QUOTE

"It is no surprise that a region as rich in natural splendor and resources as Appalachia would, from early on, attract settlers, in particular those who sought not just bounty from the land but also a more meaningful relationship with it."

—*The Appalachians: America's First and Last Frontier*

CHAPTER 6
Natural Resources and Tourism

The Appalachian Mountains are rich in natural resources including timber, coal, iron ore, and deposits of granite and marble. These resources contribute to the economic development of cities and towns within the Appalachians. Millions of tourists also visit the Appalachians each year.

Recreation

The Appalachian Mountains are one of the most popular recreational areas in all of North America. Motoring, hiking, camping, fishing, skiing, whitewater rafting, and **spelunking**, or cave exploring, are popular activities throughout the Appalachians. Many people also visit the numerous craft centers and historic sites, along with the Appalachian Trail and the Blue Ridge Parkway, which stretches 469 miles (754 km) from the Shenandoah National Park in northern Virginia to the Great Smoky Mountains National Park.

Hiking in the Appalachian Mountains is a great adventure. Planning and preparation are important for an enjoyable and safe mountain hike.

Logging Industry

Lumber and wood **pulp** industries were important parts of the economic growth within the Appalachians. In the early 1900s, before there were protected national forests, logging companies such as the Ritter Lumber Company, cut down vast areas of untouched forests in the Appalachians. Today, the Appalachian lumber industry is a multi-million dollar industry, employing 50,000 people in Tennessee, 26,000 in Kentucky, and 12,000 in West Virginia alone.

Coal Mining

When most people think of the Appalachian Mountains, they think of the coal mining industry. The region's huge coalfield covers 63,000 square miles (160,000 square km) between northern Pennsylvania and central Alabama, mostly along the Cumberland Plateau and the Allegheny Plateau. As of 2004, almost 50,000 people were working in the coal mining industry.

Clearing Land

Deforestation to clear land for planting crops and to supply people with firewood, paper, and construction materials, has slowly crept up steeper and higher slopes of the Appalachians, leading to environmental **degradation**. Deforestation is the removal of forests or an area of trees.

At a coal mine in the Appalachians, freshly dug coal is hauled up on a conveyor belt to load onto trains.

Mountaintop
mining produces
about three billion
dollars worth of
coal each year.

Manufacturing

The manufacturing industry in the Appalachians began with the iron and steel mills in Pittsburgh and in the **textile**, or woven knit cloth, mills that were established in North Carolina's Piedmont region the mid-19th century. The construction of iron and steel mills greatly increased after the Civil War. There was a manufacturing boom from 1890–1930, and many people moved from small farms and rural areas to large urban centers.

Appalachian Conservation

The Appalachian Mountain Club (AMC) promotes the protection, enjoyment, and understanding of the mountains, forests, waterways, and trails of the Appalachian Mountain region. The AMC upholds that these resources have genuine worth and also provide recreational opportunities, spiritual renewal, and ecological and economic health for the region. They believe that successful conservation depends on people becoming actively engaged with the outdoors, so they encourage people to experience, learn about, and appreciate the environment.

The AMC is the oldest outdoor recreation and conservation organization in the United States.

Ready, Set, March!

For decades, coal companies have been blasting off the tops of mountains to extract the coal that lies beneath. They then dump the rubble into the river valleys below. Unlike strip mines on the Great Plains, where miners must restore the land after they take the coal, and unlike the Appalachian's **shaft mines**, which leave the surface undisturbed, mountaintop mines destroy the region's landscape and pollute its water. In June of 2011, the United Mineworkers of America (UMWA), the largest **union** representing coal miners, joined forces with environmental and community advocates who are seeking to end mountaintop-removal coal mining. Both groups marched to historic Blair Mountain in an effort to protect the mountain from mountaintop mining.

Hundreds of people joined to protest and draw attention to the mining threats to Blair Mountain.

A haze of pollution is visible above the Great Smoky Mountains.

Preserving Resources

People need to protect the natural resources in the Appalachians for future generations to enjoy. Air and water pollution and non-native species have had a significant impact on natural resources. For example, air pollution and very acidic fog have had negative impacts on Appalachian forests from North Carolina to Canada. Air pollution damages plants and degrades the soil and waterways at high elevations. Staff members in the many national parks within the Appalachians carefully monitor threats such as air pollution and destructive non-native species and try to think of ways to preserve the valuable resources in the Appalachians.

Cars, power plants, and industry cause most of the air pollution in the Appalachians.

This foggy forest in the Great Smoky Mountains National Park was attacked by the non-native Balsam Woolly Adelgid, causing many of the trees to die.

NOTABLE QUOTE

"While habitat degradation from mountaintop mining is what one sees on the surface, we found that chemical effects are quite pronounced and limit much of the expected biodiversity from what were once naturally rich, diverse Appalachian stream systems."

—Gregory Pond, *aquatic biologist with the Environmental Protection Agency*

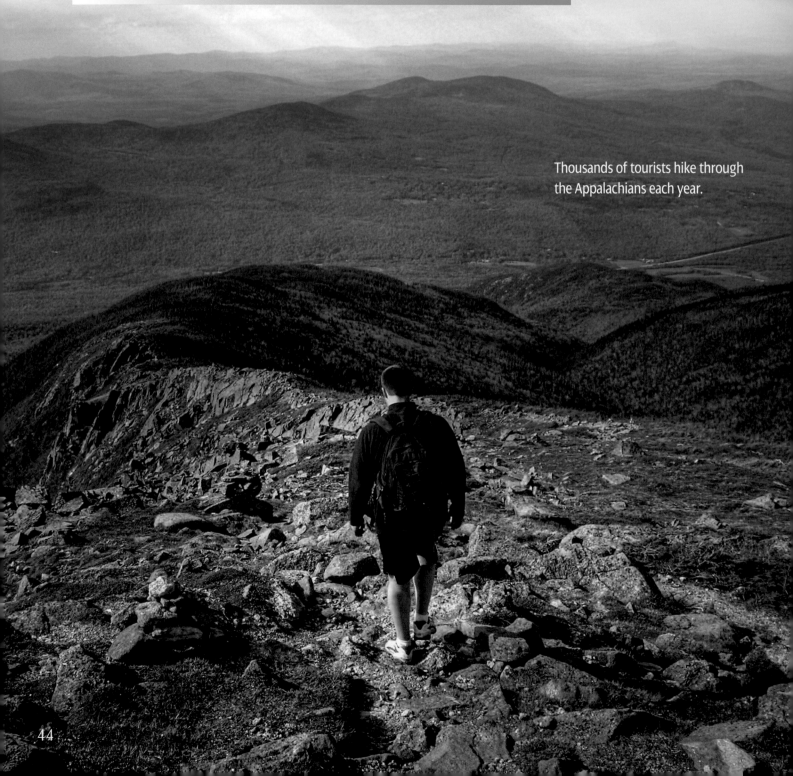

Too Many Tourists

Millions of people visit the Appalachians each year and scientists have only just begun to understand the environmental impacts of this amount of tourism. They are working hard to better understand the impacts of tourism on the Appalachian's **ecosystems** and what it means for the future of the Appalachians.

Thousands of tourists hike through the Appalachians each year.

44

Carolina Northern Flying Squirrel

There are many endangered and threatened plant and animal species in the Appalachians. The Carolina northern flying squirrel is just one endangered species. This squirrel does not truly fly, but glides through the air by out-stretching large folds of skin attached to its sides between the front and hind feet. They live in conifer and northern hardwood forests, which have been heavily impacted by the woolly adelgid. The insect kills adult trees, which means the squirrels have fewer places to make nests and find food.

The southern flying squirrel, shown here, lives in the Appalachian Mountains and closely resembles the endangered Northern flying squirrel.

TIMELINE

470–480 million years ago	Appalachian Mountains begin to form
270 million years ago	Tectonic plates carrying Africa and North America collide
10,000 years ago	The last ice age occurs
8000 B.C.	Paleo-Indians are living in the Appalachians
1500s	The first European settlers and explorers enter the Appalachians
1539	Hernando de Soto enters the Appalachian region
Early 1800s	Gold is discovered in the Appalachians
1830–1840	The United States government passes the Indian Removal Act, which forces all the Native people to move. More than 60,000 Cherokee, Chickasaw, Choctaw, Creek, and other Native people are forced to leave their traditional territories.
1876	The Appalachian Mountain Club is founded by Edward Pickering and 33 other outdoor enthusiasts
1923	First section of the Appalachian Trail opens to the public
1934	Great Smoky Mountains National Park is established
1950	A terrible storm blows through the Appalachians. More than one million people lost power and more than 300 people died in the storm.
1998	The Department of Energy estimates that there is 28.5 billion tons (25.9 billion metric tons) of anthracite coal beneath the Appalachians
2001	Elk are released into the Great Smoky Mountains National Park
2011	United Mineworkers of America (UMWA) joins forces with environmental and community advocates seeking to end mountaintop-removal coal mining

GLOSSARY

adapted Changed so as to fit a new or specific use or situation

American Revolution The war of 1775-1783 in which the American colonists won independence from British rule

basin A large, hollow area containing water

bedrock The solid rock lying under soil and other materials

carrion Dead or decaying flesh

climate The long-term weather conditions in an area

coastal plain An area of flat, low-lying land next to a coast

colonists People who live in a colony; A colony is an area of land ruled by another country and is occupied by settlers from that country.

commerce The buying and selling of goods

crystallize To cause to form crystals

decomposing Breaking down

degradation Making or becoming worse

descendants People who come from an ancestor or particular group of ancestors

dormant Not active

economy The use of money and goods and their arrangement

ecosystems Large areas of land or water containing a geographically distinct group of species, natural communities, and environmental conditions

elevation Height above sea level

ephemerals Plants that last a short time

evaporates Changes into vapor from a liquid state

folklore Customs, beliefs, stories, and sayings handed down from one generation to the next

global warming The gradual increase in Earth's temperature

hydroelectricity Electricity produced by waterpower

igneous rocks Rock that formed from lava or magma; one of the three main types of rocks on Earth

indigenous Living things that are naturally found in a particular region or environment

infestation A quantity of something that is large enough to be harmful

invertebrates A large group of animals that do not have backbones

lava Melted rock that comes from a volcano

leaf litter Dead or decaying leaves

mammoths A large species of elephant that is extinct

metamorphic rocks Rock that changes over time; one of the thee main types of rocks on Earth

migrated Moved from one place to another

mineral A naturally occurring substance that comes from the ground

natural resources Materials found in nature that are valuable or useful to humans

nutrients Materials that living things need to survive

omnivores Animals that feed on both plants and other animals

oxygen A colorless, tasteless, odorless gas, which forms about 21 percent of the atmosphere and is necessary for life on Earth

pigments Substances that give color to other materials

pulp A material from wood that is used to make paper

shaft mines The deepest underground mines

spelunking Exploring caves

subarctic Describing regions that border on the Arctic zone

supercontinent A former large continent, from which other continents broke off and drifted away

tectonic plates Gigantic pieces of Earth's crust

textile Woven or knit cloth

timber Wood that is used to make something

trough A long and narrow hollow

union A group formed by combining parts or members

INDEX

FIND OUT MORE

BOOKS

Frome, Michael. *Strangers in High Places: The Story of the Great Smoky Mountains*, Expanded Edition. University of Tennessee Press, 1994.

Maynard, Charles W. *The Appalachians (Great Mountain Ranges of the World)*. Powerkids Press, 2004.

Weidensaul, Scott. *Mountains of the Heart: A Natural History of the Appalachians*. Fulcrum Publishing, 2000.

WEBSITES

Appalachian National Scenic Trail (U.S. National Park Service) www.nps.gov/appa/index.htm

U.S. National Park Service www.nps.gov/index.htm

Appalachian Mountain Club www.outdoors.org/

National Geographic: Discover Appalachia www.nationalgeographic.com/appalachia/

WWF Global 200 Ecoregions–Appalachian and Mixed Mesophytic Forests www.nationalgeographic.com/wildworld/profiles/g200/g069.html